Copyright 2021 by JAZZY HARMONY

Adult coloring book

COFFEE

skilfully pictured in everyday situations. Stacked coffee cups, coffee at the computer, coffee and flowers, take away coffee held in hands and so on...

Coloring book zen

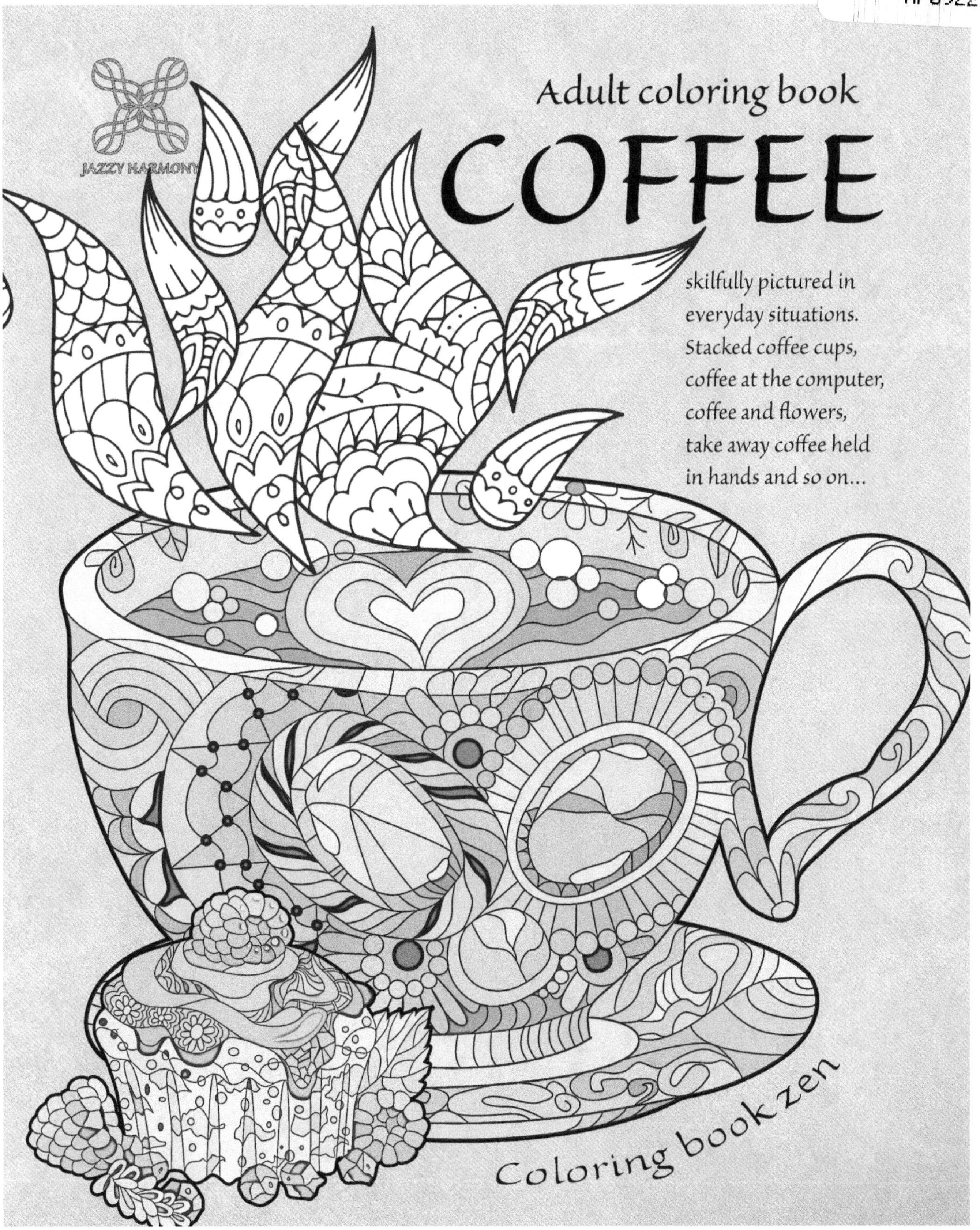

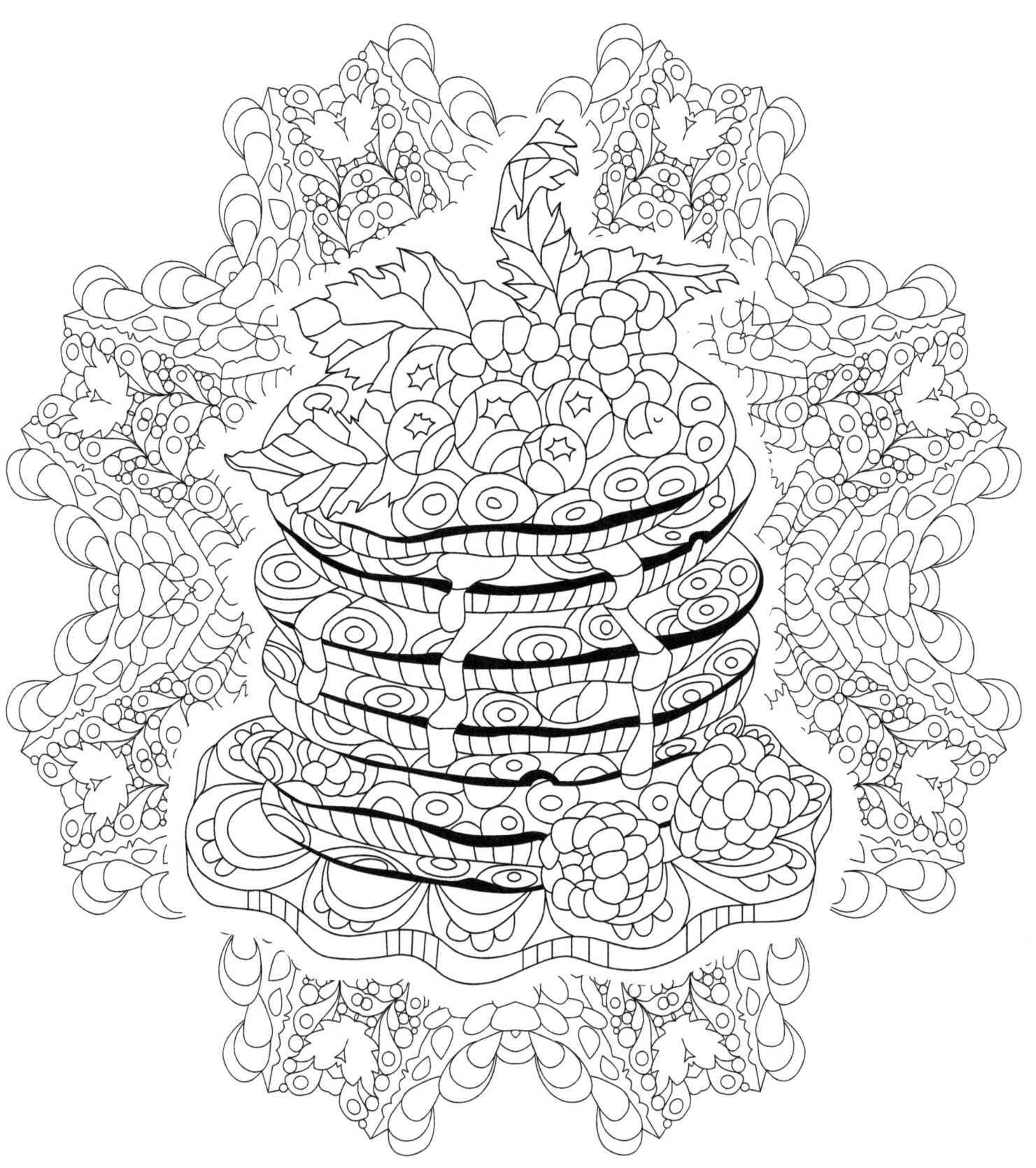

More coloring books by Jazzy Harmony available on AMAZON

GRAFFITI

CRAZY

A Crazy street art coloring book for teens and adults

Adult coloring book

JAZZY HARMONY